101 Things Not To Do While Smoking Weed

This book is dedicated to all
the real smokers, dabbers,
and vapors. It is for
entertainment purposes only
but can be very helpful so
enjoy and tell a friend.

1

Be stingy.

Share is caring so don't be
stingy or greedy.

Never chip in.

Don't be that dude. At least
bring snacks.

3

Wet the blunt or joint up.

Nobody wants your germs
dude. Torch it if u have to
make sure its dry.

4

Anything unproductive.

Getting high from marijuana
gets the creative juices
flowing. Don't waste this by
just sitting around

Hold a conversation while holding the blunt or joint.

Are you getting paid by the hour to babysit that blunt? Puff puff pass dumbass.

Be unappreciative .

If you did not chip in be thankful . Even if u did chip in be kind.

Eat seafood.

No one wants to smoke your
tuna breath.

Address your parole officer.

Just stay away from cops in general.

Pick up your kids from a hostile ex.

It will be a waste.

Tell your landlord the rents going to be late.

For some reasons people associate weed with being lazy .

Drop the blunt or joint.

If you drop the blunt/joint you
pass it. If you drop and break
the bong. You pay for it.

12

Argue

Again, it is a waste of weed.

13

Crack

Just say no to drugs.

Send a work email.

It will be full of errors.

15

Job interviews.

Smoke afterwards. As a
reward of a job well done.

Think smoking and eating edibles are the same.

Edibles may take a while longer to hit you but boy when they do!

Let your pipes get filthy or cloggy.

No one wants to smoke out of
a toilet bowl.

Thinking you can just eat a bud and get high.

You have to heat weed to get high.

Underestimate
the dab.

It will tackle you.

20

Be wasteful.

Cherish the weed. Don't
abuse her.

Throw out the doobies.

Save those doobies for a rainy day.

Pack a sloppy bowl.

Use a grinder. Get your life together.

Roll a sloppy blunt.

Sometimes sloppy blunts are okay as long as they hit well.

Claim it's laced.

Don't claim it's laced because you can't handle. Go to the bathroom, throw some water on your face , drink some milk, and calm your simple ass down.

Use a torch.

Unless you're dabbing. There
is no need for a torch. You
will look like a crackhead.

Put someone else's lighter in your pocket.

For some reason the human brain is wired to automatically put lighters in pockets. Try to fight this animalistic urge.

Store it in bad places.

Weed should be in glassed
jars If u asked me but never
ever just leave it out to dry.

28

Throw out the stems.

Make a tea, hash or
something. You can even use
it for a wick.

Light the filter.

Please check if the joint you
are about to smoke has a filter
on the tip. If so light the other
end.

Smoke it like a cigarette.

Again I say weed is to be cherished.

Dab naked.

Dabbing naked is like frying bacon naked. You're going to hurt yourself.

Answer the door without looking.

This is common knowledge. I shouldn't have to explain this.

Listen to music with police sirens.

How about we just stop making music with sirens period.

Peer pressure.

It's not cool to pressure anyone. Let's bring an end to this.

Jokingly yell "cops."

No one finds this funny.

Mess up the rotation.

So that nothing gets confused
just pass it to the left.

Blow smoke directly in someone's face.

That's very disrespectful and may cause a fight. That is not what stoners are about.

Be a fiend.

Take your crackhead
tendencies else where. This is
a stoners assemble.

Light if you didn't roll it.

If you don't roll it you don't get the 1st hit unless you are granted permission from the roller.

Smoke too fast.

This isn't a race and we don't want to make the blunt/joint runny so don't do it.

41

Vomit.

Like I said some people react
differently to weed so if you
just happen to vomit don't
keep smoking.

Blow others high.

If you are having some type of
issues that may effect others.
Just smoke alone.

43

Make a business call.

You may think you sound
smart when you're high but
you sound stupid af.

Have a panic attack.

Weed tend to hit different people in different ways if you do have a panic attack don't be afraid to let a friend know.

45

Go to court.

Don't give other stoners a bad
name by doing some dumb
shit an alcoholic would do in
the name of Mary Jane.

Get drunk.

If your going to drink and
smoke just drink to get a buzz.
Getting drunk is just a waste
of weed.

Bogart.

Sharing is caring but hogging
is bothering. Puff puff pass!

48

Skip Rotation.

This is a crucial violation.
Always remember to pass to
the left unless you're in a car.

Go to church.

Them church going folks don't
want to smell unless you smell
like holy water so hold off on
the anointment and reward
yourself for sitting threw that.

Be stingy.

Don't be stingy if you have enough to share. Sharing is what the stoner's community is about.

Drive a manual.

Operating heavy machinery is a no-no while intoxicated but some of us been smoking since the age of 12 and know what we are doing. Well driving a stick while smoking is too difficult ,

Grocery shopping.

Unless you have eaten don't go grocery shopping. You will build a lot of useless junk food.

Go to the police station to pick up a friend who got a DWI.

We have all don't it but Its really not a good idea to bail a friend out smelling like the inside of Willie Nelson's pocket.

Drive at night during a snow storm.

You don't want to waste your high on this nerve wrecking adventure.

Watch the news.

It will just amplify your paranoia.

Passers must be met halfway.

When passing: passer reaches as far as they feel comfortable. Receiver must cover the remaining distance. You want it? Come get it.

Someone's significate other.

Keep your genital on the loyal route. It's better for everyone.

Sleep.

Don't waste a good high by falling asleep. Do something productive or watch a movie.

Become a troll.

It's never cool to be a troll.
Just be yourself.

Spill the bong.

Be careful when handling someone's bong. Treat with care.

Eat saltine crackers.

That shit will kill you!

Eat a spoon of cinnamon.

That shit will kill you twice.

Count cash, especially people's cash .

Get your own money.

Get lost.

Don't go for a scroll down
unfamiliar territory.

Interact with law enforcements.

Just don't ever talk to ops.

Assume your partner in crime wants to have sex with you.

Sometimes others just want
to relax and enjoy their high.

Pass someone's product to a person they don't know.

If it's not your product don't invite unwanted guest to the party.

Look for anything.

You won't find it.

Pick your nose.

That's just gross.

Pass to right.

Always pass to the left. It's universal law.

Ash on floor.

Unless it's your floor. Have
some respect and use a
ashtray. If you can't find one
get creative and make one out
of a cup or something.

Streak.

A marijuana high may make
you want to get naked but
please try to resist or just stay
inside your own home.

Pass a bowl full of ash.

If you pass an empty bowl
please at least notify the
receiver.

Complain about someone's roll.

Someone took the time and
roll and blunt/joint for you.
Show some appreciation.

Spit in the bong.

It doesn't matter if it was by mistake. No one wants to look at a bong and see saliva running down it.

Take more than two puffs per turn.

If u didn't contribute just take
two puffs and pass it.

Take a lighter
from a man's lap.

Pause.

Pass an ashy blunt/joint.

Ash before you pass please.

Open the window
of a hotbox.

Number 1 rule to hotboxing is
to keep the smoke contained.

Scratch balls.

Again, that's gross.

Fart during hotbox session.

Again my friend, gross.

Hide anything.

You wont ever see it again.

Get people sick.

If you have the flu please some by yourself. This is the one time where being selfish is cool.

Let another stoner die.

If you're hosting the session
make sure your friends are
hydrated and not starving.

Assume people smoke tobacco.

Not everyone can handle the harshness of a blunt or backwood so show some courtesy.

86

Let the joint canoe.

Don't let the blunt get
running. Take soft delicate
pulls to prevent this.

Tell people how many edibles to eat.

No one likes The Edible Police
so be kind and mind your
business.

Pass an
uncleared bong.

Never pass a bong full of
smoke. Someone could of
gotten high from all the
smoke you wasted by passing
it.

Talk about getting busted.

Don't talk about unwanted
scenarios .Unless you want
them to happen.

Start a brush fire in California.

Pot smokers already get enough slack from the masses about being dimwitted don't fall into this stereotype.

Be disrespectful.

Again be appreciative and
common courtesy when in
someone else's pad.

Smoke a cigarette.

Again do assume because
someone smokes weed that
they smoke cancer sticks too.

Pinch from friends.

Stealing from friends just isn't cool. Ever!

Talk about the harms of smoking marijuana.

Nobody wants to hear that shit.

Visit in-laws.

Unless you want your high to
get blown.

Change diapers.

Smoking around kids isn't cool.

Bring negativity.

Positive vibes only stony.

Break bongs.

If you break it you pay for it.

Be embarrassed
if you cough.

Cough is a good thing as long
as you're sick.

Drink bong water.

No one wants to see that. Not even cool. Gross!! I'm embarrassed for you.

Post your smoking habits online in states where its illegal.

1st off no one cares so why brag and get yourself unwanted attention.